UGH! HOW *TASTELESS*!!

What's the difference between a hormone and an enzyme?
(see page 94)

Why did God create men?
(see page 66)

Where do female airline pilots sit?
(see page 122)

What was the first thing Adam said to Eve?
(see page 13)

What's the function of a woman?
(see page 84)

What do you call a comedian whose underwear is too tight?
(see page 28)

What's a perfect 10?
(see page 75)

Blanche Knott's
Book of Truly Tasteless Anatomy Jokes

VOLUME I

SMP

ST. MARTIN'S PAPERBACKS

BLANCHE KNOTT'S BOOK OF TRULY TASTELESS ANATOMY JOKES

Copyright © 1990 by Blanche Knott.

ISBN: 0-312-92062-8

Printed in the United States of America

First St. Martin's Press mass market edition/February 1990

10 9 8 7 6 5 4 3

to Matthew and Megan, bodies beautiful

PART ONE: MALE ANATOMY

A man came into a saloon, and soon after he'd sat down at the bar he noticed a horse in the back of the room with a big pot of money in front of it. "What's that all about?" asked the newcomer.

"You gotta put a dollar in the pot," explained the bartender, "and you collect all the dough if you can make the horse laugh."

At that the man went over to the horse, whispered something in its ear, and the horse cracked up. It was still rolling on the floor as the man walked out the door with the pot under his arm.

Five years went by and the same man found

himself in town again. Deciding to visit the bar, he encountered the same horse in the same spot with another big pot of money in front of it. "Well?" he asked the bartender, who didn't look any too pleased to see him.

"It's not so easy, this time, pal," cautioned the bartender. "You gotta make the horse cry."

The fellow walked over to the horse, and within a minute the horse was on its knees, sobbing as though its heart were breaking. He picked up the pot and was on his way out when the bartender stopped him. "I know the money's yours, buddy, but can't you at least tell us how you did it?"

"Sure," he said with a grin. "Nothing to it. The first time I told him my prick was bigger than his, and the second time I showed him."

•

Henderson was enjoying a few at his local pub when a man joined him at the bar, swaying back and forth as he stood there. It started to get on Henderson's nerves, so finally he turned to the stranger and asked, "What's with all this lurching back and forth? Can't you stand still?"

"I was with the Merchant Marine for nineteen years," the fellow explained genially, "and the roll of the sea kind of got in my blood."

"Is that so? Well, I've got fourteen kids,"

sputtered Henderson, starting to pump his hips energetically back and forth at the bar, "and I don't stand like this!"

•

What's long and hard and full of semen?
 A submarine.

•

The nudist colony offered woodworking as one of the activities, so Mike decided to try his hand at it. He was busy whittling away when his knife slipped and almost cut off his penis.
 "Jesus, Mike," shrieked his pecker, turning to look up at him, "we've had our share of fistfights, but I never thought you'd pull a knife on me!"

•

What did the egg say to the boiling water?
 "How can you expect me to get hard so fast —I just got laid a minute ago!"

•

Terry and Larry go to the movies. "Gee, you're cold tonight," she whispers.
 Larry hisses back, "You're holding my popsicle."

•

The routine practice of circumcision was part of a certain small-town doctor's job, and he found himself reluctant to discard the foreskins. So he saved them all up in a jar of formaldehyde. Many years went by and the doctor decided to retire, and as he was cleaning out his office he came across the jar, which by this time contained hundreds of foreskins. Again it seemed a pity to throw them away, especially after all this time. So the doctor took the jar to the tailor shop around the corner. "Say, can you make something with these?" he asked.

"No problem," replied the tailor cheerfully after assessing the contents of the jar. "Come back in a week." And a week later he proudly presented the doctor with a beautiful wallet.

"Now wait just a minute," protested the doctor. "It's very nice, but there were literally hundreds of foreskins in that jar. All I get to show for them is a measly *wallet*?"

"Calm down, Doc," the tailor said reassuringly. "Rub it a little bit and it turns into a suitcase."

•

The only survivor of a shipwreck, Pierre washed ashore on a desert island. He managed to find food and water, and didn't mind the solitude, but he grew horny as hell. So when a sheep walked down the beach one day, he dragged the beast back to his hut and jumped it. But just as he was starting to get it on, a dog ran out of the jungle and began to attack him, and in trying to defend himself from the dog, Pierre had to let the sheep go.

In the weeks that followed, the sheep appeared regularly, but every time Pierre tried to get romantic with her, the dog materialized and attacked him viciously.

Weeks and months went by and Pierre grew hornier and hornier, until his salvation appeared: a lovely young woman washed up on the shore. She was half drowned, but Pierre was able to resuscitate her, and when she came to, she was grateful beyond words. "You saved my life," she sobbed. "I would have drowned. How may I repay you? I'll do anything, just name it. . . . Anything!"

"Okay," commanded Pierre. "Hold that dog."

•

What was the first thing Adam said to Eve?

"Stand back—I don't know how big this thing's gonna get!"

•

Harry noticed he was running low on rubbers, so he stopped by the local drugstore. "What size?" asked the pharmacist's assistant sweetly.

When he admitted he wasn't sure, she led

him into the back room, lifted her skirt, and told him to enter her. He was glad to obey.

"Size six," she informed him after a moment or two. "Take it out. How many please?"

Harry bought a dozen, and on the way down the street he ran into his friend Alan, to whom he eagerly recounted the whole episode. Needless to say, Alan rushed right in to place an order. "I'm afraid I don't know my size," he told the salesgirl.

So she led him into the back room and repeated the procedure. "Size seven, sir, take it out. How many, please?"

But Alan plugged away, undeterred, until he'd shot his wad. "None, thanks," he told her, zipping up. "Just came in for a fitting."

•

What do you get when you cross a rooster with a peanut-butter sandwich?

A cock that sticks to the roof of your mouth.

•

And when you cross a rooster with an owl?

A cock that stays up all night.

•

Farmer Swenson came into town for market day and sold everything but one goose by noon, so he decided to treat himself to an afternoon at the movies. But the girl at the ticket counter took one look at the goose and said, "You can't take that bird in here."

Swenson went around the corner, stuck the bird under his belt, and headed into the theater. Everything was fine through the first couple of gunfights, but eventually the goose started getting restless. So Swenson took pity on it and opened his fly so the bird could stick its head out for some fresh air.

Two little old ladies sitting next to the farmer were also enjoying the matinee.

"Minnie," whispered one to the other, "you seen one, you seen 'em all—but this one's eating my popcorn!"

●

The horny midget found that the best way to make time with women was to be direct about it. So he went up to the tallest, blondest woman at the party and said, "Hey, honey, whaddaya say to a little fuck?"

She looked down at him and replied, "Hello, you little fuck!"

●

A black couple took their young son for his first visit to the circus, and by chance their seats were near the elephants. When his father got up to buy some popcorn, the little boy piped up, "Mom, what's that long thing on the elephant?"

"That's the elephant's trunk, dear," she answered.

"I know *that*. The other thing."

"Oh, you mean the elephant's tail," she said helpfully.

"No, Mom. Down underneath."

His mother blushed. "Oh, that's nothing, honey," she told him, and changed the subject.

Pretty soon the man returned with the popcorn and the woman went off to buy a soda. As soon as she had left, the boy turned to his father and repeated his question.

"That's the elephant's trunk, son," answered his father with an indulgent smile.

"Dad, I *know* what an elephant's trunk looks like. I'm talking about the other end."

"Why, that's his tail."

"No, Dad. Down *there."*

After taking a good look, the father sat up and explained, "That's the elephant's penis, son."

"Gee, Dad," piped up the kid, "how come when I asked Mommy, she said it was nothing?"

The father took a deep breath and a smile came over his face. "Son," he explained, "I've *spoiled* that woman."

•

Hector decided to treat himself to a trip to the whorehouse, and turned to catch the hooker's expression when he dropped his pants—his dick was eighteen inches long.

"Oh, my God," gasped the poor girl, "you're not putting *that* inside me! I'll kiss it, I'll lick it . . ."

"No way," Hector broke in. "I can do that myself."

•

Heard the new Webster's definition of "small"?

"Is it in yet?"

•

The Bergs needed a new car, so they went to the nearby Oldsmobile dealership to pick one out. No sooner had gorgeous Mrs. Berg set foot on the car lot than the salesman's jaw dropped. He couldn't take his eyes off her.

Never one to pass up a chance at a bargain, Berg pulled the salesman aside and commented on his appreciation of his wife's charms. "She's really something, eh?" he commented with a sly smile.

The salesman nodded dumbly, eyes glued to Mrs. Berg's cleavage.

"Tell you what," Berg proposed. "You've got a back room here, right? Let's take her back there, and if you can do everything I can do,

17

I'll pay double for the Olds convertible over there."

The salesman agreed enthusiastically, his gaze dropping to Mrs. Berg's perfect, mini-skirted ass. As soon as the door was closed, Berg pulled up his wife's T-shirt and started fondling the luscious melons that popped out. The salesman followed suit energetically.

Next Berg circled her navel with his tongue. The salesman licked her whole stomach, try-ing not to drool.

Next Berg pulled up her teeny-weeny skirt, feeling the soft down of her inner thighs. The salesman followed suit, the slight tang of her pussy almost driving him insane.

Next Berg pulled out his pecker and folded it in half.

The salesman sighed. "What color car d' you want?"

•

Why does a dog lick his balls?
Because he can.

•

"Doc," said LaRusso, "I got nine kids and the wife's expecting again. How do I stop the stork?"

The doctor replied, "Shoot it in the air!"

•

A certain Polish couple wanted a baby more than anything in the world, but all their efforts came to nothing. One day they were out for a stroll when they spotted a black couple pushing their beautiful new baby in a stroller. Going over and admitting their heart's desire, the Poles shyly asked the other couple if they had any advice.

"There are a few tricks to it," conceded the black man. "For one thing, you gotta be eight inches long."

"No problem," said the Pole.

"Secondly," the new father went on, "you gotta be at least three and a half inches around."

"So *that's* the problem," exclaimed the other fellow, turning to his wife with a huge smile. "We've been letting too much light in!"

•

What does a man have in his pants that a woman doesn't want in her face?
Wrinkles!

•

What do you have when you've got two little green balls in your hand?
Kermit's undivided attention.

•

Bill was pretty naive when it came to sex, so he decided to pay a visit to the local prostitute. But no sooner had he been shown into her room and taken down his pants than he shot his wad.

"Too bad, sonny," commiserated the hooker. "Can you come again?"

"Oh, no problem," Bill told her cheerfully. "I live right in the neighborhood."

•

A young man had always been plagued with insecurities about the size of his endowment. Deciding to take matters into his own hands, he went to a doctor and announced his desire to have his penis surgically enlarged.

The doctor checked things out and informed the patient that the only real surgical possibility was to implant a section of baby-elephant trunk.

Rather radical, agreed the young man, but he was adamant in his desire to proceed with the operation, whatever the risk. The surgery went off without a hitch, and after a month of recuperation, the man decided it was time to try out his new equipment in the field.

He asked a lovely young woman of his acquaintance out to dinner at an elegant restaurant. They were enjoying appetizers and quiet conversation when his new organ, which had been comfortably resting in his left pants leg, whipped out over the table, grabbed a hard roll, and just as speedily disappeared from sight.

"Wow!" exclaimed his date, clearly impressed. "Can you do that again?"

"Sure," answered the fellow, "but I don't know if my asshole can stand another hard roll."

•

José cracked up when he came home and found his wife ironing her brassiere. "Why bother?" he asked, wiping tears of laughter off his cheeks. "You got nothing to put in it."

"Is that so?" she shot back. "I iron your shorts, don't I?"

•

Did you hear about the masochist who said to her boyfriend, "Give me nine inches and make it hurt"?

So he screwed her twice and slapped her.

•

A woodpecker from North Carolina flew up to the Catskills for his summer vacation. He went to work on his first lodge-pole pine, *rat-tat-tat-tat-tat*, when a bolt of lightning struck the tree and split it right down the middle.

"God *damn* it," grumbled the woodpecker.

"It never fails to astound me how hard my pecker gets when I'm away from home."

•

It was time for sex-education class, and the teacher asked the class, "Children, who can tell me what breasts are?"

"My mommy has breasts," piped up Rhonda, "two of them."

"Right you are," praised the teacher. "And who can tell me what a penis is?"

"Me, me," piped up Eric. "My daddy has two of them."

"Oh, really? Are you sure about that, Eric?"

"Yup. One's about this long," the little boy told her, holding his hands about four inches apart, "and looks like mine, and the other one's about this long," holding his hands about seven inches apart, "and he uses it to brush Mommy's teeth with."

•

After the birth of his third child, Warner decided to have a vasectomy. During the operation, one of his testicles accidentally fell on the floor, and before the nurse could scoop it back up, the doctor had stepped on it. Unfazed, the doctor simply asked the nurse for a small onion, which he proceeded to suture inside the scrotum.

Two weeks later Warner was back for his

post-op checkup. "How's it going?" asked the doctor.

"I gotta tell you, I'm having some problems," admitted the patient.

"Such as?"

"Well, Doc, every time I take a leak, my eyes water; every time I come, I get heartburn; and every time I pass a Burger King, I get a hard-on!"

•

What's hard and straight going in, soft and sticky coming out?

Chewing gum.

•

When Ernie walked into the pharmacy and asked for rubbers, the girl behind the counter asked politely, "What size, please?"

"Gee, I don't know," answered Ernie, a little flustered, so she instructed him to use the fence out back to determine the correct size. And as he walked out the back door, she ran out a side door, around, and behind the fence.

The fence had three holes in it.

Putting his penis in the first hole, Ernie felt capable hands gently stroking it. Reluctantly, he pulled it out and inserted it in the second hole, and within seconds he felt a warm, wet pussy at work on the other side of the fence. Groaning with pleasure, he managed to pull out and stick it through the third hole. There an expert set of lips and tongue gave him the blowjob of his dreams.

Jumping up, the salesgirl hurried back behind the counter and was standing there smiling when Ernie staggered back through the door. "Your size, sir?" she asked politely, taking no notice of his disheveled state.

"Forget the rubbers," he gasped. "Just gimme three yards of that fence."

●

Three guys were having an argument about who was more generously endowed. Finally, to settle the matter once and for all, they went up to the top of the Empire State Building and proceeded to unzip their flies.

"Pretty good, eh?" Mort's cock was hanging all the way down to the fifty-seventh floor.

"Take another look," Bill told him, waving his dick across a window on the fortieth floor. "I got you beat cold."

He looked smugly over at the third man and was startled to see him doing a sort of jig, jumping from one foot to the other and peering anxiously over the edge of the observation deck. "Harry, what the hell're you doing?" he asked.

Wiping the sweat off his forehead, Harry replied, "Dodging traffic."

●

When O'Connor went in for his physical, he confessed that his sexual performance wasn't all it could be. "Haven't you got any medication that could help me out?"

The doctor hemmed and hawed, but finally pulled out a vial of small blue pills. "These should do the trick," he told his patient, dismissing him.

"Boy, you weren't kidding," yelled O'Connor into the phone a few hours later. "Three times already!"

"Fine, fine," nodded the doctor, smiling. "And your wife, she's happy, I hope?"

"I don't know," admitted the grateful patient. "She's not home from work yet."

•

How is a man like a snowstorm?

Because you don't know when he's coming, how many inches you'll get, or how long it'll stay.

•

Ohrenstein was less than pleased with the doctor's remedy for the constant fatigue that was plaguing him. "Give up sex completely, Doctor?" he screamed. "I'm a young guy. How can you expect me to just go cold turkey?"

Leaning back in his chair, the physician suggested, "So get married and taper off gradually."

•

Two guys were sitting on a bridge passing the time of day over a six-pack, and pretty soon they both had to take a leak. Wanting to impress his companion, the first guy whistled. "Gee, this water's cold."

"Yup," agreed his companion. "And deep."

•

Philip and Michael were live-in lovers. One day Philip called in sick, and Michael called home in the middle of the morning to see how he was feeling. "Oh, by the way," he asked, "did the paperboy come yet?"

"No," answered Philip, "but he's got that glassy look in his eye . . ."

•

What's twelve inches long and white?
Nothing.

•

When the traveling salesman got the message at the hotel desk that his wife had given birth, he rushed to the phone. "Hi, honey," he cried happily. "Is it a boy or a girl?"

"Irving, Irving," sighed his wife wearily, "is that all you can think about? Sex, sex, sex?"

•

Having married a virgin, the newlywed husband wished to take special pains to make sure her sexual inexperience wouldn't be the cause of any trouble in their relationship. Taking her into his arms that first night, he explained that he didn't ever want her to feel pressured into having sex with him, that it should always be a matter of her own free will.

"In fact, darling," he went on tenderly, "I think we should set up a little system so there will never be cause for a misunderstanding between us." He looked deep into her eyes. "Here's how it'll work: when you want to have sex, pull my penis once; when you don't want to, pull it a hundred times."

•

When the doctor pulled down Johnson's pants, he was shocked to discover that his penis was a mangled wreck. "Jesus!" he couldn't help exclaiming. "What the hell happened to you?"

Despite his pain, Johnson blushed. "I had a real good thing going, Doc," he explained. "See, the girl who lives next to me in the trailer park was widowed not too long ago. When she gets lonely, she takes a knothole out of the floor, puts in a hot dog, and goes to work squatting over it. So I figured to myself, why not get in on the action?" A dreamy look came over Johnson's face.

"And then?" prodded the doctor.

"Everything was going great until last night," said Johnson, wincing. "Then some son of a bitch rang the doorbell and she tried to kick the hot dog under the stove."

•

What did the Pole do before going to the cockfight?

Greased his zipper.

•

Why's it so easy to turn on Frankenstein's monster?

Because he has amps in his pants.

•

What's the difference between "ooh" and "aah"?

About three inches.

•

What would you call a comedian whose underwear was too tight?

Dickie Smothers.

•

One night after their proprietor had fallen asleep, the parts of the body were arguing about which had the toughest job. "I've really got it rough," complained the feet. "He puts me in these smelly sneakers, makes me jog till I'm covered with blisters . . . it's brutal."

"You've got nothing to complain about," maintained the stomach. "Last night I got nothing but bourbon, pizza, and aspirin. It's a miracle I'm not one big ulcer—yet."

"Oh, quit bitching, you two," moaned the penis. "Every night, I'm telling you, he sticks me in a dark tunnel and makes me do push-ups until I throw up."

•

Joe and Moe went outside to take a leak and Joe confessed, "I wish I had one like my cousin Junior. He needs four fingers to hold his."

Moe looked over and pointed out, "But you're holding *yours* with four fingers."

"I know," said Joe with a sigh, "but I'm peeing on three of them."

•

What do you get when you cross a rooster and a telephone pole?

A thirty-foot cock that wants to reach out and touch someone.

•

Mort knew he was probably oversensitive about the problem, but the fact was that his eyes bulged out. He went to doctor after doctor, but none seemed to know of any treatment, and in desperation he looked up "Eyes Bulging Out" in the Yellow Pages. Sure enough a doctor was listed, and a few days later Mort found himself sitting on a vinyl couch in a seedy waiting room. A little nervous about being the only patient, he reminded himself how rare the condition was and that the doctor *was* a specialist.

At long last he was admitted to the doctor's office and examined. The doctor leaned back and informed him that there was a remedy, but not an easy one. "I must cut your balls off," he informed the prospective patient.

Mort's eyes bulged out even more as he headed for the door. But after a few weeks of thinking it over, Mort admitted that his bulging eyes were what was keeping him from getting laid in the first place, so he decided to go ahead with it. So he returned to the doctor's office, and sure enough, after the operation his eyeballs sank back into their sockets most agreeably. In fact, he looked not only normal, but actually rather handsome.

Delighted, he thanked the doctor profusely, and decided to treat his remodeled self to a new suit. "Charcoal-gray pinstripe," he instructed the tailor. "Medium lapel, no cuffs."

"Fine," said the tailor, nodding. "Come back on Tuesday."

"Aren't you going to measure me?" asked Mort.

"Nah. I've been at this over thirty years; I can tell your size just by looking," the tailor assured him.

"That's impossible," insisted Mort.

"Size forty-two jacket, right?"

"Yes," admitted Mort, surprised.

"Thirty-two-inch inseam, right?"

Mort nodded, amazed.

"Thirty-six-inch waist?"

Again Mort nodded, dumbstruck.

"And you wear size forty underwear, right?" concluded the tailor with a smile.

"Nope!" Mort retorted. "Thirty-four."

"Listen, you can't fool me," said the tailor wearily. "Don't even try."

"I'm telling you, I wear size thirty-four underwear," Mort insisted.

"You *can't* wear size thirty-four underwear," protested the exasperated tailor. "Your eyes would bulge out of their sockets!"

•

Did you hear about the man who couldn't spell?

He spent the night in a warehouse.

•

A certain couple loved to compete with each other, comparing their achievements in every aspect of their lives: salaries, athletic abilities, social accomplishments, and so on. Everything was a contest, and the husband sank into a deep depression because he had yet to win a single one.

Finally he sought professional counsel, explaining to the shrink that while he wouldn't mind losing once in a while, his unbroken string of defeats had gotten him pretty down.

"Simple enough. All we have to do is devise a game which you can't possibly lose." The shrink thought for a moment, then proposed a pissing contest. "Whoever can pee higher on the wall wins—and how could any woman win?"

Running home, the husband called upstairs, "Darling, I've got a new game!"

"Ooooh, I love games," she squealed, running down the stairs. "What is it?"

"C'mon out here," he instructed, pulling her around to the patio. "We're going to stand here, piss on this wall, and whoever makes the highest mark wins."

"What fun! I'll go first." The woman proceeded to lift her dress, then her leg, and pee on the wall about six inches up from the ground. She turned to him expectantly.

"Okay, now it's my turn," said the beleaguered husband eagerly. He unzipped his fly, pulled out his penis, and was just about to pee when his wife interrupted.

"Hang on a sec," she called out. "No hands allowed!"

•

There was once a pro football player called Smithers, whose main role was warming the bench. Before every game he would put on his pads and uniform, smear his cheeks with charcoal, don his helmet, and run out onto the field with the rest of the team. But play after play, game after game, season after season went by without Smithers ever being called into action.

One Saturday night near the end of the season, Smithers was feeling lousy. "Helene," he said to his long-time girlfriend, "I want you to do me a favor. Dress up in my uniform, smear your face, put on my helmet, and sit on the bench for me this game. You know I never play, so no one'll ever know the difference."

Helene wasn't too keen on the idea, but she finally agreed, and the next Saturday found her sitting on the bench. Sure enough, no one on the team gave her a second look, and the first half passed without event. During half-time she hung around the locker room, the third quarter went on by, and it wasn't till the last quarter that one man after another started falling to injuries. The bench grew emptier and emptier, and finally the desperate coach barked, "Smithers, get in there!"

Utterly panicked, Helene went out onto the field, crouched down in the lineup, and was knocked out cold within the first three seconds of play. When she came to, she found herself on a cot in the locker room, the coach vigorously massaging her pussy. "Don't worry, Smithers," he said nervously, "once we get your balls back in place, your cock'll pop right up."

•

Jack was delighted by the opportunity to use the golf course at the swank country club, even more so when he hit a hole-in-one on the eighth hole. As he bent over to take his ball out of the cup, a genie popped out. "This club is so exclusive that my magical services are available to anyone who hits a hole-in-one on this hole," the genie explained. "Any wish you desire shall be granted."

"How about that!" Jack was thrilled, and immediately requested a longer penis.

"Your wish is granted," intoned the genie solemnly, and disappeared down the hole in a puff of scented smoke.

The golfer went on down the green, and as he walked, he could feel his dick slowly lengthening. As the game progressed, Jack could feel it growing and growing, down his thigh, out from his shorts leg, down past his knee. "Maybe this wasn't such a great plan after all," muttered Jack to himself, and headed back to the eighth hole with a bucket of balls. Finally he managed a hole-in-one, and when he went to collect the ball, he had to hold up the head of his penis to keep it from dragging on the ground.

Out popped the genie, saying, "This club is so exclusive that my magical services are available to anyone who hits a hole-in-one on this hole. Any wish you—"

"Yeah, yeah, yeah," interrupted Jack. "Could you make my legs longer?"

•

Why can't you circumcise an Iranian?

There's no end to those pricks.

•

A man walked into a bar and started up a conversation with an attractive woman. Pretty soon he confided that he was recently divorced. "My wife and I just weren't sexually compatible," he explained. "I wanted to experiment, you know, try new things, but my wife just wasn't into it. Nice girl, but totally traditional."

The woman's eyes widened as she listened to this tale of marital incompatibility. "That's pretty amazing," she said. "I got divorced a year ago myself, for the same reason. My husband was a total stick-in-the-mud when it came to experimenting sexually." Dropping her voice to a whisper, she confessed to her new acquaintance, "he didn't even like me to be on top."

"Wow, this is *great!*" exclaimed the guy. "You and I are really on the same wavelength. What do you say we go back to my place and get it on?"

"Fine by me."

Back at his apartment he issued very specific instructions. "Here's what I want you to do. Take off all your clothes, climb up on my bed, get on your hands and knees, and count to ten."

She obeyed exactly. "Ten," she called out, tingling with excitement. Nothing happened. "Yoo-hoo . . . ten," she called sweetly. Then, "I'm waiting . . ."

"Jeez, I'm sorry," blurted the guy. "I got off already. I just shat in your purse."

•

What's the definition of conceit?

A mosquito with a hard-on floating down the river on his back and yelling, "Open the drawbridge!"

•

The voluptuous blonde was enjoying a stroll around Plato's Retreat, arrogantly examining everyone's equipment before making her choice. In one room she happened against a scrawny, bald fellow with thick glasses, and to complete the picture, his penis was a puny four inches in length.

Checking it out with a sneer, the blonde snickered, "Just who do you think you're going to please with *that?*"

"Me," he answered, looking up with a smile.

•

Why did the tenor hire a hooker?
He wanted someone to hum his parts.

•

What has a thousand teeth and eats wienies?
A zipper.

•

An international conference of sexologists was convened to determine once and for all why the penis is shaped the way it is. Each national delegation had done extensive research and was to present its results.

Said the French spokesman, "We have spent five million francs and can now definitively state zat ze penis ees zat shape in order to give pleasure to ze woman."

"I beg to disagree," opined the British representative. "We've spent thirty thousand pounds and are quite sure that the shape is such that maximum pleasure is felt by the man."

"We've spent a million bucks," drawled the American scientist, "and there's no doubt about it: it's that shape so your hand doesn't slip off the end."

•

One day Tommy went into the local tattoo parlor with a somewhat odd request. He had this great new girlfriend named Wendy, he explained, and while their sex life was dynamite, he was sure it would be even better if he had her name tattooed on his prick.

The tattoo artist did her best to dissuade him, pointing out that it would be very painful, and that most of the time the tattoo would just read "Wy" anyway. But Tommy was undeterred, and insisted on going ahead with it. Sure enough, Wendy was crazy about the tattoo, and their sex grew even wilder and more frequent. Tommy was a happy man.

One day he was downtown and had to take a leak in a public bathroom. At the next urinal was a big black guy, and when Tommy looked over, he was surprised to see "Wy" on this guy's penis as well. "How about that!" he exclaimed. "Say, is your girlfriend's name Wendy too?"

"Dream on," said the black guy. "Mine says, 'Welcome to Jamaica and Have a Nice Day.'"

•

What's the dumbest part of a man?

His prick. (It's got no brains, its best friends are two nuts, and it lives next door to an asshole.)

•

What do you get when you sleep with a judge?

Honorable discharge.

•

When Paddy O'Brian died, Father Flanagan was there to comfort the bereaved widow. "You know, Molly, the whole community is here to help you through this time of sorrow," he consoled her, "and of course if there's anything I can do, you know I will."

Parting her veil and drying her tearstained cheeks, the widow whispered a single request in the priest's ear. Father Flanagan blushed scarlet and refused outright, but the widow persisted, and finally he gave in to her pleading. Saying, "Give me twenty-four hours," he left. And the next day he showed up at the

O'Brian house with a parcel wrapped in brown paper.

The widow popped the contents into a pot on the stove, and as it was boiling away, a neighbor dropped by. "I say, Molly," commented the neighbor, opening the lid, "isn't that Paddy's penis?"

"Indeed it is," confirmed Molly. "All his life I had to eat it his way, and now I'm eating it mine."

•

Eve and Lola were comparing notes. "I just adore French men," Lola confessed.

"But they're so arrogant and domineering," protested Eve, "and always making jokes at a woman's expense."

"True, all true," admitted Lola with a smile, "but they always eat their words."

•

What three two-letter words can best dampen a man's ardor?

"Is it in?"

•

Why did the football team beat off in the huddle?

Because the coach had told them to pull themselves together.

How can a real man tell if his girlfriend's having an orgasm?

Real men don't care.

•

For Christmas Freddy got the chemistry set he'd been begging for, and he promptly disappeared with it into the basement. Eventually his father came down to see how he was doing, and found Freddy, surrounded by test tubes, pounding away at the wall.

"Son, why're you hammering a nail into the wall?" he asked.

"That's no nail, that's a worm," explained Freddy, and showed his dad the mixture in which he'd soaked the worm.

"Tell you what, pal," suggested Freddy's father, his eyes lighting up. "Lend me that test tube and I'll buy you a Toyota."

Needless to say, Freddy handed it over, and the next day when he got home from school he spotted a brand-new Mercedes Benz in the driveway. "Hey, Dad, what's up?" he called, running into the house.

"The Toyota's in the garage," explained his father, "and the Mercedes is from your mom."

•

A woman sought the advice of a sex therapist, confiding that she found it increasingly difficult to find a man who could satisfy her and that it was very wearisome getting in and out of all these short-term relationships. "Isn't there some quicker and easier way to judge the size of a man's endowment?" she asked.

"The only foolproof way," counseled the therapist, "is to judge by the size of his feet."

So the woman headed downtown and proceeded to cruise the business district until she came across a young man with the biggest feet she'd ever laid eyes on. She invited him to dinner, flattered him wildly, and took him back to her apartment for a night of passion.

When the man woke the next morning he found the bed next to him empty. On the bedside table was $40 and a note that read, "With my compliments, go out and buy a pair of shoes that fit you."

•

What comes after 69?
   Listerine!

•

What does a guy with a twelve-inch dick have for breakfast?
   Well, this morning I had scrambled eggs, whole-wheat toast, and a cup of coffee. . . .

•

After asking the starlet to strip, why did the producer take off his own clothes?

He wanted to see if she could make it big.

•

What do you get when you cross a penis and a potato?

A dicktater.

•

The newly divorced forty-five-year-old made an appointment with a urologist and told him he wanted to be circumcised. "Most women seem to prefer it," he explained, "and now that I'm dating quite a bit, I'd rather not worry about it."

The arrangements were made, and when the patient woke up from the surgery he saw the doctor standing by the bed with a very contrite expression on his face. "I've got good news and bad news," he admitted. "The bad news is that the knife slipped."

"Oh, my God," gasped the patient. "What the hell's the good news?"

"It isn't malignant!"

•

Hear about the guy who got his vasectomy at Sears?

Every time he gets a hard-on, the garage door goes up.

•

Little Jack Horner sat in the corner
Fondling his dick and his balls.
  Along came his mother,
  Who scolded, "Oh, brother—
You better get that off the walls."

•

What's the difference between anxiety and panic?

Anxiety is the first time you can't do it a second time, and panic is the second time you can't do it the first time.

•

(Note: for this joke you need a long-necked beer bottle as a prop.)

A young woman was out on a date and couldn't seem to come up with anything to talk about but her old boyfriend—his hobbies, his car, his habits. (Stroke the length of the bottle lovingly during this part of the joke.)

Finally the new man in her life grew exasperated. "You're always going on about him!" he exploded. "How about thinking about *me* for a change."

"You've got a point," she admitted. (Move

44

your hand up to stroke just the neck of the bottle.) "I'll try."

·

This 600-pound guy decides he can't go on living like a human blimp, so he seeks the advice of a clinic and goes on a drastic diet. It works; four months later he's down to 160 and feeling great. There's just one problem: he's covered with great folds of flesh where the fat used to be.

His doctor tells him not to worry. "We've got a special surgical procedure to correct the problem," the doctor reassures him. "Just come on over to the clinic."

"But Doctor," protests the one-time fatty miserably, "I'm too embarrassed to go out in public like this. I really look weird."

"Don't give it another thought," says the doctor. "Just pull all the flesh as high as it'll go, pile it on top of your head, put on a ski hat, and come on over."

Dying of self-consciousness, the patient follows these instructions, but mercifully arrives at the front desk of the clinic without provoking any comments. "The doctor will be right with you," the receptionist tells him with a friendly smile. "Say, what's that hole in the middle of your forehead?"

"My belly button," blurts the guy. "How d'ya like my tie?"

What's six inches long, has a head on it, and makes women go wild?

Folding money.

•

Hear about the flasher who decided to retire?

Yeah, but then he changed his mind and decided to stick it out another year.

•

What's the definition of a bachelor?

A man who prefers to ball without the chain.

•

A guy found a tarnished brass lamp lying on the beach one day. Being an optimistic sort, he rubbed it a few times, and to his delight a genie materialized. "Your command, my lord?" prompted the spirit, bowing low. "You may have your heart's desire."

Without a second's hesitation, the man put in his request. "I want a penis that touches the ground."

So the genie cut his legs off.

•

One afternoon the red phone on Prime Minister Thatcher's desk rang.

Gorbachev was on the line, asking an urgent favor. "The AIDS virus has reached the USSR, and we are suffering from an acute condom shortage. In fact," the premier confessed, "there are none at all to be had in the Moscow pharmacies. Would it be possible for you to ship me 850,000 condoms—immediately—so that we can deal with this public health threat?"

"Why certainly, Mikhail," replied Mrs. Thatcher gracefully. "Will Friday do?"

"That would be wonderful," sighed the Russian in evident relief. "Oh, and Maggie, one specification: they must be five inches around and nine inches long."

"No problem at all," the Prime Minister assured him breezily.

Hanging up, she had her secretary get the largest condom manufacturer in Great Britain on the line, who informed her that a rush order to those specifications would be no problem for his assembly line. "Excellent, excellent," chirped Thatcher. "Now just two more things . . ."

"Yes, madam?"

"On the condoms must be printed, 'Made in Great Britain,'" Thatcher instructed.

"But of course," the industrialist assured her.

"And 'Medium.'"

•

Why did the rubber fly across the room?
It got pissed off.

•

What do you give to the man who has everything?
Penicillin.

•

What's the only thing the government can't tax?
A penis, because 95% of the time it's inactive, 5% of the time it's in the hole, and it's got two dependents and they're both nuts.

•

"Doctor," the man told his physician, "I need a new penis."

The doctor took the request completely in stride. "No problem," he told his patient. "We have a five-incher, a seven-and-a-half-inch model, and a nine-incher. Which do you think would be right for you?"

"The nine-incher," the man decided on the spot. "But would it be possible to take a look at it first?"

"Of course," said the doctor obligingly.

"Gee, Doctor," asked the patient after a few moments, "could I have it in white?"

•

Vance couldn't understand why Pete didn't want to come along with the guys to check out some XXX-rated movies. "C'mon, pal," he urged. "Vera even said she'd give you the night out."

Finally the henpecked husband admitted the truth. "It just gets to me, Vance," he groaned, "to see a guy having more fun in ten minutes than I've had in the last twenty years."

•

Jake and Jim were about to head out for another long winter trapping in the northernmost wilds of Saskatchewan. When they stopped for provisions at the last tiny town, the proprietor of the general store, knowing it was going to be a good many months without female companionship, offered them two boards featuring fur-lined holes.

"We won't be needing anything like that," Jake protested, and Jim shook his head righteously. But the storekeeper pressed the boards on them, pointing out that they could always be burned as firewood.

Seven months later, bearded and gaunt, Jake walked into the general store. After a little chitchat about the weather and the price of pelts, the storekeeper asked where his partner was.

"I shot the son of a bitch," snarled Jake. "Caught him trying to use my board."

•

A young man was spending the night at the apartment of a married couple of his acquaintance. As there was no couch, the couple offered to share their own bed with the guest, and they all retired early.

Not long afterward the wife whispered in the young man's ear, "Pull a hair from my husband's butt; if he's asleep, we can make love."

Surprised but not displeased, the young man did as instructed. Getting no response from the husband, he proceeded to make it with the wife. Not completely satisfied, the wife proposed the same course of action a second time, and later a third time, and the young guest was only too happy to oblige. His ardor was dimmed, however, when the husband rolled over and confronted the couple. "Look," he said wearily, "it's bad enough that you're screwing my wife in the same bed—but do you have to use my ass as a scoreboard?"

•

What do you call a man who weeps while he's masturbating?

A tearjerker.

•

There once was a bodybuilder who had to take a wicked piss, so he knocked a couple of people over on the way to the bathroom. When he finally got there, both urinals were occupied, so he tossed the nearest offender out the window. With a sigh of relief he quickly unzipped his fly, pulled out his eleven-inch cock, and began to urinate. Turning to the guy next to him with a smile, he said, "Whew, I just made it."

Frankly impressed, his neighbor said, "Wow —will you make me one too?"

•

Why's a penis like Rubik's Cube?
The more you play with it, the harder it gets.

•

Jack and Jill went up the hill to fetch a pail of water, but Jack fell down and got hurt. Early the next day, Jack was complaining about the sharp pain in his groin, so Jill brought him to the emergency room for an examination. Only a few minutes into the doctor's examination, Jill left the room and ran all the way home.

"What happened?" asked Mom when Jill burst into the kitchen.

"Mom, Mom, Jack was masturbating!"

"Really," asked Mom in a concerned tone.

"Yeah," said Jill. "The doctor took hold of his balls and said, 'Jack, cough.'"

An inquisitive young man was on a flight to Hawaii and was having a number of drinks to help get him in the vacation spirit. Quite perturbed to discover that the men's room was under repair, he asked the stewardess for admittance to the ladies' room. "Certainly," said the stewardess graciously, "as long as you don't touch the buttons marked WW, PP, and ATR."

Rather desperate, the young man readily agreed, but no sooner had he relieved himself than his curiosity got the better of him. Pressing the WW button, he enjoyed the sensation of warm water being sprayed up onto his rear end. This was so pleasant that he barely hesitated before depressing the PP button, and was rewarded by the soft pat of a powder puff on his bottom. Much emboldened, he pushed the button marked ATR.

He felt a searing pain, and the next thing he knew, he was waking up in a bright, white room with a nurse standing by his bedside.

"You pushed the WW button, right?" she asked with a knowing look in her eye.

"Yes," the young man admitted.

"And the PP button?"

The man nodded.

"And then you pushed the ATR button, am I correct?"

"Yeah, so?"

"ATR stands for Automatic Tampon Removal," explained the nurse. "By the way, your penis is on your pillow."

•

What's the definition of a tough competitor?

In a jack-off competition, he finishes first, third, and ninth.

•

How about the definition of a jockstrap?

An All-American ball carrier.

•

What's the difference between a dick and a magic lantern?

If you rub a dick three times, the genie isn't going to be the one to come.

•

What do a cobra and a two-inch dick have in common?

No one wants to fuck with either of them.

•

Garry was chuckling at the bar when his friend Steve joined him. "Women, they think they're so smart," he said with a sly smile, going on to explain that he'd eavesdropped on a phone conversation between his fiancée and her best friend. "She said, 'Garry doesn't know it yet, but the only time I'm putting out is when I want to get pregnant.'"

At this Garry doubled over with laughter, and Steve looked at his friend with some consternation. "I'd be pissed as hell—why aren't you?" he asked.

"Why get mad?" answered Garry. "She'll *never* know I've had a vasectomy."

•

Why shouldn't you go down on a twelve-inch cock?

You might get foot-in-mouth disease.

•

Heard anything about the "morning-after" pill for men?

It works by changing your blood type.

•

One morning old Pa Jones informed his ancient wife that he was planning a trip into town that day to apply for Social Security. "But Pa," she said, "you don't have a birth certificate. How're you going to prove your age?"

"Now don't you worry, Ma." Giving her a little pat, Pa headed out. Sure enough he was back in a few hours with the news that the first check would be along within three weeks.

"So how'd you prove your age, eh?" asked his wife.

"Easy," said Pa with a smile. "I just unbuttoned my shirt and showed 'em all the gray hairs on my chest."

"Well while you were at it," scolded the old woman shrilly, "why didn't you drop your pants and apply for disability?"

•

Swallowing his pride, Fred finally made an appointment with the great foreign specialist and told him he wanted his penis enlarged. After examining him, the doctor prescribed a bottle of pills. "Each time you take one, say 'Wee,'" the doctor instructed him solemnly, "and your penis will actually grow."

Fred was barely out of the parking lot before he popped ten of the pills. Unfortunately the twitching of his growing penis excited him so much that he lost control of the car. As it plunged over a cliff his squeal of terror—"Weeeeeeeeeeeeeee"—rang out loud and clear.

Not long afterward a couple was driving down the same road. "Look, honey," observed the woman, "there's the hairiest telephone pole I've ever seen."

•

What's worse than a fellatrix with overbite?
A cunnilinguist with five-o-clock shadow.

Why do women have more trouble with hemorrhoids than men do?

Because God made man the perfect asshole.

●

What's the difference between light and hard?
(1) It's light all day.
(2) You can sleep with a light on.

●

One day a construction worker left the job a little early, and when he got home he found his wife in bed with another man. Purple with rage, he hauled the unfortunate offender down the stairs and out to his workshop in the garage, where he proceeded to secure the offender's penis in a vise. Utterly terrified, the man screamed, "Stop! *STOP!* You're not going to cut it off, are you? *ARE YOU?!?*"

"Nope," the construction worker answered with a gleam in his eye, "you are. I'm going to set the garage on fire."

●

What's the difference between a snowman and a snow woman?

Snowballs.

●

What's worse than a piano out of tune?

An organ that goes flat in the middle of the night.

•

One spring day two men were out hunting. Feeling a sudden need to relieve himself, George went over to a nearby clump of bushes and started to pee. Suddenly a poisonous snake lunged out of the greenery and bit him right on the end of his dick.

Hearing George's howl of pain and fright, his friend Fred rushed over. "Lie still," he urged the victim. "I'll run to town for a doctor."

Luckily, the doctor in the nearest town was in his office. "There's only one way to save your friend's life," the doctor advised gravely. "If you cut an X over the snakebite and suck all the venom out, he'll probably live."

Fred got back in the pickup and not much later reached the clearing where George lay. Raising himself weakly on one elbow, George cried, "Fred, Fred, what'd the doctor say?"

"George, old friend," replied Fred sorrowfully, "he said you're gonna die."

•

Why do women have such big tits and tight pussies?

Because men have such big mouths and little peckers.

What do you do in case of fallout?

Put it back in and take shorter strokes.

•

A few days before his proctological exam, a one-eyed man accidentally swallowed his glass eye. At first he was worried, but when there seemed to be no ill effects, he forgot all about it.

Once in the doctor's office, the man followed instructions, undressed, and bent over. And the first thing the proctologist saw when he looked up the man's ass was the eye staring right at him.

"You know," he said, coming around the table to confront his patient, "you've really got to learn to trust me."

•

What do you get when you cross a stud with a debtor?

Someone always into you for at least ten inches.

•

What does the IRS have in common with rubbers?

Both stand for inflation, halt productivity,

and cover up a bunch of pricks—and most people can see right through them.

●

What can Life Savers do that a man can't?
   Come in five different flavors.

●

The big black man had been convicted of rape and sentenced to death, and finally the day came around. A murmur rippled through the audience when his pants leg was slit open at the knee for placement of an electrode, revealing the head of his penis.
   "Don't say nuthin', gentlemen," said the condemned man gravely. "If you was gonna be electrocuted, you'd be all small and shriveled up too."

●

Graffiti: "I'm ten inches long and three inches wide. Interested?"
Reply: "Fascinated. How big is your dick?"

●

Why aren't cowboys circumcised?
   So they have someplace to put their chewing tobacco while they're eating.

●

A man walked into a ladies' room and casually unzipped his fly. "Sir," chastised a female patron severely, "this is for *ladies!*"

"Don't worry sugar," he assured her with a smile, "so's this."

•

How far could you see if you had a twelve-inch prick growing out of your forehead?

You couldn't see at all because the balls would be in your eyes.

•

A certain man was plagued with a run of bad luck. When he picked his shirt up out of the drawer, all the buttons fell off. When he tried to leave the room, the doorknob came loose in his hand. When he bent down for his brief-case, the handle came right off. And for three days he was afraid to take a leak.

•

"Doc, you gotta help me," said Mr. Smith, walking into the physician's office. "I need a prescription for Sex-lax."

"Don't you mean Ex-lax?" asked the doctor.

"No, no, no," answered Smith testily. "I don't have trouble going, I have trouble coming."

•

After a pleasant dinner and movie, the guy drove the girl back to her apartment. Stopping his car in front of the building, he pulled out his cock and placed her hand on his crotch. She promptly slapped him with the other hand, jumped out of the car, stomped up to her front door, and turned around to yell, "I've got two words for you: *drop dead!*"

"And I've got two words for you," he screamed back. *"LET GO!!!"*

•

If our ancestors came over on a boat, how did herpes get here?

On the captain's dinghy.

•

What's the definition of macho?

Jogging home from your own vasectomy.

•

The proud father gave his son twenty bucks on his sixteenth birthday and sent him off to the local whorehouse. His grandmother's house was on the way, and when she beckoned him inside to wish him happy birthday, he explained where he was off to. She insisted that he save the money and make love to her.

The boy returned home with a big smile on

his face. "It was great, Dad, and I saved the twenty bucks," he reported.

"How's that?" asked his father.

"I did it with Grandma."

"What!" screamed his father. "You mean you screwed my mother?"

"Cool out, Dad, why not? You've been sleeping with mine."

•

At her annual checkup, the attractive woman was told by the new doctor that it was necessary to take a rectal temperature. The patient agreed, but a few minutes later protested, "Doctor, that's not my rectum!"

"And it's not my thermometer," admitted the doctor with a grin.

At that moment the patient's husband, who had come to pick her up, came into the examining room. "What the hell's going on in here?" he demanded, taking stock of the situation.

"Just taking your wife's temperature," explained the doctor coolly.

"Okay, doctor," said the man grudgingly, "but that thing better have numbers on it."

•

What's the lightest thing in the world?

A penis. Even a thought can raise it.

Once there was a woman who couldn't get enough, so she put an ad in the paper. The next afternoon a man came to her front door, and she asked him to pull down his pants. "I'm sorry, buddy," she explained as she showed him out, "but it has to be six feet long. Come back in a week."

A week passed and the doorbell rang again. It was the same fellow. "Hmmm . . . two feet. Come back in a week and we'll see what we can do," murmured the woman.

Another week went by, and when the doorbell rang she found the man with his dick wrapped around his neck. "Not bad," conceded the woman, "but you've still got a foot to go."

"Hold on a sec," asked the man. "I brought a crank with me." Inserting his penis, he finally stretched it out to a full six feet.

"Okay, fella," she said with a smile. "Come on back to my room." Upstairs, she stripped down to a flimsy negligee and turned to her guest with a smile.

So the man got a hard-on and strangled himself.

•

What's been the most effective means of birth control since the days of Adam and Eve?

Laughter.

•

Three old men were sitting around talking about who had the worst health problems. The seventy-year-old was plagued by urinary problems. "Every morning I get up at 7:30 and have to take a piss, but I have to stand there for an hour 'cause my pee barely trickles out," he complained.

"Heck, that's nothing," said the eighty-one-year-old. "Every morning around 9:30 I have to take a dump, but I'm so constipated I have to sit on the can for an hour. It's terrible."

"You think *you* have problems!" moaned the ninety-two-year-old. "Every morning at 7:30 I piss like a racehorse, and at 8:30 I shit like a pig. The trouble is, I don't wake up till eleven."

•

The sergeant put his troops through a fancy drill, at the end of which they lined up three rows deep. Walking down the line, the sergeant stopped in front of each soldier, whacked him on the chest with his baton, and barked, "Did that hurt, soldier?"

"No, *sir!*" each replied.

"Why not?" yelled the sergeant.

"Because I'm in the U.S. Army, *sir!*" came the reply.

Continuing on, the sergeant saw a huge penis sticking out of the line and proceeded to whack it with his baton. "Did that hurt, soldier?" he boomed.

"No, *sir*," answered the private.

"And why not?"

"Because it belongs to the guy behind me, *sir!*"

•

A playboy stepped into a bar looking for some action and was delighted to see a gorgeous blonde walk in. To his dismay, she walked right past him and cosied up to a dirty old alcoholic nursing a whiskey in the corner. Five minutes later he cheered up when a lovely redhead entered the bar, but she too headed straight for the derelict's table.

At a loss, the stud leaned across the bar and beckoned for the bartender. "What's with that old coot?" he asked.

"Got me," admitted the bartender with a shrug, "though I've been watching him for a while now. All I know is he comes in every day, orders a shot of the house whiskey, sits in the same seat, and licks his eyebrows."

•

One night this guy got so bombed that he went from the bar to the local tattoo parlor. There the tattoo artist listened carefully to his instructions and tattooed "I Love You" on his dick.

The next night he and his wife were going down on each other when she suddenly went wild with rage. "What's the matter, honey?" he asked tenderly.

"I cook for you, I clean for you, I do everything for you," she screamed, sitting bolt upright, "and now you're trying to put words in my mouth!"

•

Why did God create men?

Because you can't get a vibrator to mow the lawn.

PART TWO:
FEMALE ANATOMY

A young man was brought up by his father in the Australian outback. Not wanting the boy to get into trouble, the father told him to stay away from women. "They have teeth down there," he explained, and let the impressionable young boy's imagination do the rest.

Eventually, however, the old man died, and seeing his acquaintances getting married and starting families, the young man decided it was time to get on with it. So he rode into the nearest town and found himself a willing girl —who was rather disappointed when the consummation of their wedding night consisted of a peck on the cheek. The second night she dolled herself up in a sheer negligée, only to have her new husband again kiss her on the cheek, roll over, and fall fast asleep. On the third night she caught him before the snores began and proceeded to give him a brief lecture on the birds and the bees and his conjugal duties.

"Oh, no you don't!" he cried, sitting up in alarm and pulling the bedclothes tightly around himself. "I know about you women! You've got teeth down there, and I'm not coming anywhere near!"

Being a good-humored sort, his bride roared with laughter, then invited her husband to come around and see for himself. Warily he circled the bed and proceeded to check out her anatomy with great care. Finally he stuck his head up.

"You're right," he proclaimed. "You've got no teeth, and your gums are in terrible condition!"

•

What does an elephant use for a tampon?
A sheep.

•

Did you hear why Polish women don't use vibrators?
They chip their teeth.

•

What's the difference between parsley and pussy?

Nobody eats *parsley*.

•

It was a hot summer day in the ghetto, and a bunch of little kids were sitting out on the front stoop with no money, nowhere to go, nothing to do. Finally Leroy's father stuck his head out the window, tossed his kid a buck, and told the kids to get lost.

Leroy dashed off down the block, the others following after him, and they were very surprised when he disappeared into the corner drugstore. In a few minutes he emerged carrying a small brown bag. "What's in the bag?" clamored his friends, crowding around him eagerly.

They were less than pleased when he pulled out a box of Tampax. "Hey, man," they groaned collectively, "we wanted to go out an' buy ourselves a good time with that money. What'd you go an' buy *that* shit for?"

"That's why I *got* it," Leroy explained with a big smile. "It says right here on the box: you can go swimming, you can go horseback riding . . ."

•

How can you tell a Pole designed the lower half of a woman's anatomy?

Who else would put the snack bar so close to the shithole?

•

Know how these days everyone wants a second opinion?

Well, this lady had been going to a psychiatrist for years, and one day she decided she'd had enough of it. Walking into his office, she announced, "Doctor, I've been seeing you every Thursday for five years now. I don't feel any better, I don't feel any worse. What's the story? I want you to level with me—what's wrong with me?"

"I'll tell you then," said the doctor. "You're crazy."

"Now wait just a minute," protested the woman. "I'm entitled to a second opinion."

"Okay," offered the doctor obligingly. "You're ugly, too."

•

Why do tampons have strings?

So you can floss after you eat.

•

What's red and has seven little dents in it?

Snow White's cherry.

•

This guy walked into a bar and said to the bartender, "I'll have a scotch and soda . . . and get that douche bag whatever she'd like, on me." He motioned at a young woman sitting at the far end of the bar.

"Listen, buddy," said the bartender, "this is a family place, and I'll thank you not to use that sort of language in here."

"Right, right," said the customer. "Just get me that scotch and soda, and get the douche bag a drink."

"Now see here," sputtered the bartender, "that's a perfectly nice girl, and—"

"I'm getting thirsty," interrupted the guy, "and hurry up with the douche bag's order too."

Giving up, the bartender walked over to the young woman and rather shamefacedly said, "The gentleman over there would like to offer you a drink—what'll you have?"

Beaming, she answered, "Vinegar and water, please."

•

Know why women have cunts?
So men will talk to them.

•

A couple was making out in the back seat and things were getting pretty hot and heavy. "Put your finger inside me, baby," instructed the girl, and the guy was only too happy to oblige.

"Put another finger inside me," she ordered, moaning in pleasure.

"Put your whole hand inside me."

"Put both hands inside me."

"Now clap."

"I can't!" he protested.

"Tight, huh?" she said with a smile.

●

How do you fuck a fat girl?

Roll her in flour and go for the wet spot.

●

"Ya got no tits and a tight box," snarled the biker to his girlfriend.

"Get off my back!" she snapped.

●

Why do women slap Polish midgets?

Because they're always telling them how nice their hair smells.

●

Did you hear about the blind gynecologist?

He could read lips.

●

The newly engaged couple was necking in his car and things started getting pretty steamy. "Oh darling, darling," the girl gasped at last, "kiss me where it smells."

So he drove her to New Jersey.

●

Why did God create women?
Because sheep can't cook.

●

What's a perfect 10?
A woman three feet high with no teeth and a flat head you can rest your beer on.

●

So what's a Cinderella 10?
A woman who sucks and fucks till midnight and then turns into a pizza and a six-pack.

●

Harry came into work on Monday feeling absolutely fine, and so was astonished when his secretary urged him to lie down on the sofa. He was even more so when his boss took one look at him and ordered him to take the day off, if not the week. Even his poker buddies wouldn't have anything to do with him that night, insisting he go back home and straight to bed. Finally, tired of resisting everyone's advice, he made a doctor's appointment. The doctor took one look at him and rushed over with a stretcher.

"But Doctor," protested Harry, "I *feel* fine."

Well, this was a puzzler, conceded the doctor, who proceeded to turn to the enormous reference books behind his desk, muttering to himself, "Looks good, feels good . . . no, you look like hell. Looks good, feels terrible . . . nah, you feel fine, right?"

Harry nodded.

Thumbing furiously through another volume, the doctor went on, "Looks terrible, feels terrible . . . nope, that won't do it either. . . . Aha—looks terrible, feels terrific." The doctor stuck his head up with a grin. "You're a vagina!"

•

What's the difference between garbage and a girl from New Jersey?

Sometimes garbage gets picked up.

•

How can you tell if your girlfriend's too fat?

If she sits on your face and you can't hear the stereo.

•

Two women were passing the time of day out on the front stoop. "Damn it all," confided one woman, "my husband came home with a dozen roses last night. I'm going to have to spend all weekend with my legs in the air."

"Whatever for?" wondered her companion. "Don't you have a vase?"

•

Why do women have two holes?

So that when they're drunk, you can carry them home like a six-pack.

•

There once was a young man who was fixated on the female breast, and eventually his problem became so acute that he decided to seek professional help. The first test his new psychotherapist performed was one of simple word association. "Just repeat after me the first word that comes into your mind," instructed the doctor. "Orange."

"Breast," replied the young man instantly.

"Plum," said the doctor.

"Breast."

"Grapefruit," said the doctor.

"Breast."

"Windshield wipers," said the doctor.

"Breast."

"Now just hold on a second," interrupted the doctor. "Oranges I can see reminding you of breasts. Grapefruits, sure. Plums, maybe. But windshield wipers?"

"Sure," explained the young man. "First this one, then that one . . ."

•

What's the difference between a bowling ball and a pussy?

You can only fit three fingers in a bowling ball.

•

A young couple was making out feverishly on the young woman's parents' sofa a few days before their wedding. "Oh, baby," moaned the groom-to-be, "please let me see your breasts. I just wanna look."

The girl blushed but unbuttoned her shirt.

"Oh, honey," he begged, "just let me kiss 'em."

"Don't you think we should wait till the wedding?" she protested, but it was already too late.

Pretty soon he was begging her to take off her panties. "I just wanna look, I swear," he panted.

"I really think we should wait till the wedding, like we said we would," said the girl, but her fiancé's frantic urging finally won her over. She was adamant that he just look, insisting that kissing her down there was something they should hold off on. But after half an hour of artful argument he had his way, burying his head between her thighs.

A few seconds later he stuck his head up. "Baby," he asked anxiously, "you think that'll keep till Saturday?"

•

What do you call a woman who can suck a golf ball through 50 feet of garden hose?

Darling.

•

This well-to-do suburban woman makes an appointment for her annual checkup with a new gynecologist. Following the examination, he ushers her into his office. "You'll be glad to hear that everything's in tiptop shape," he tells her, leaning forward with a smile. "In fact, you have the cleanest vagina I've ever seen."

"It should be," the matron snaps. "I've got a colored man coming in twice a week."

•

What's the perfect woman?

A deaf, dumb, and blind nymphomaniac who owns a liquor store.

•

It was late, and the tired cabbie was on his last run of the night. Reaching his destination, he said to his little old lady customer, "That'll be eight bucks, please."

There was no reply, and thinking she might have a hearing problem, he repeated loudly, "Lady, the fare is eight bucks."

Still no response. So he turned around, only to be greeted by the sight of the old woman hoisting her skirts and spreading her legs, no underwear impairing the view.

"Well, sonny?" she cackled. "How's this for payment?"

"Aw, lady," sighed the weary cabbie, "doncha have anything smaller?"

•

Realizing she wasn't getting any younger, the middle-aged woman decided to spice up her sex life. Since she'd always had a crush on the Beatles, she went to the local tattoo parlor with a very specific request. "I'd like John Lennon tattooed on the inside of my right thigh," she instructed him, "and Paul McCartney on the inside of my left thigh. Now, are you sure you can handle this?"

The tattoo artist assured her he was the best in the business, and set to work.

Ten days later the woman took off the bandages. She went over to the mirror in great anticipation, only to discover to her horror the two portraits bore no resemblance at all to

Lennon and McCartney. She rushed over to the tattoo parlor in a rage.

"I don't see what you're complaining about," said the proprietor soothingly. "In fact I find the likenesses quite remarkable. But obviously we need a third opinion." Out he went, coming back in with the first person he'd encountered, a wino still reeling from the night before.

The tattooist confronted him with the evidence. "Now, tell me, on the right side, does that look like John Lennon?"

"I dunno," said the wino after a long pause.

"Well, how about the one on the left? Is that, or is it not the spitting image of Paul McCartney?"

The wino thought it over for a few minutes. "I dunno," he finally offered. "But that guy in the middle with the beard and the bad breath, that's *gotta* be Willy Nelson."

•

What's the only thing used sanitary napkins are good for?

Tea bags for vampires.

•

Why does it take women longer to climax?

Who cares?

•

Three guys were sitting around in a bar one afternoon discussing whose wife was the most frigid. Harry was positive he had the worst of it. "Listen, you guys, my wife comes to bed with an ice cube in each hand, and in the morning they haven't begun to melt."

"That's *nothing*," said Phil. "My wife likes to have a glass of water on the bedside table, but by the time she's carried it in from the bathroom, it's frozen solid."

"Aw, hell," snorted Herb, "*my* wife is so frigid that when she spreads her legs, the furnace kicks on."

•

God has just spent six days creating the heavens and the earth, and since it's the seventh day, He and Gabriel are sitting back and admiring His handiwork.

"You know, God," says Gabriel, "you've done one hell of a job—pardon my language. Those snowy peaks are unbelievably majestic, and those woods, with their little sunny dells and meadows . . . masterful. Not to mention the oceans: those fantastic coral reefs, and all the sea creatures, and the waves crashing on pristine beaches. And all the animals, from fleas to elephants—what vision! Not to mention the heavens; how could I leave them out? What a touch, that Milky Way!"

God beams.

"If you'll excuse my presumption," Gabriel goes on, "I have just the teeniest question. You know those sample humans you put down in the Garden of Eden?"

God nods, a frown furrowing His divine brow.

"Well I was just wondering whether, for the obvious reason, they shouldn't have differing sets of genitalia the way all the other animals do?"

After God reflects on the matter for a minute or two, a big smile crosses His face. "You're absolutely right," He agrees. "Give the dumb one a cunt!"

•

Why do women rub their eyes when they get out of bed in the morning?

Because they don't have balls to scratch.

•

There was great excitement in the laboratory when the eminent scientist announced a new invention. "I'm calling it the 'apple,'" he announced proudly.

His colleagues lost no time in pointing out to him that the apple had been around for a long time.

"Yes, yes," interrupted the scientist impatiently, "but this apple tastes like pussy. Try it."

A willing fellow took a big bite, only to spit

it out all over the lab floor. "It tastes like *shit*," he yelled indignantly.

"Indeed," said the scientist. "Turn it around."

•

What's the function of a woman?
Life-support system for a pussy.

•

What do you call a truckload of vibrators?
Toys for twats.

•

The elementary school lesson for the day was The Farm. "All right, children," spoke up the teacher, "who can tell me the name of the big red building all the animals sleep in?"

"The barn," piped up a little girl in the front row.

"Very good, Melissa. And who knows the name of the tall building right next to the barn where the farmer stores his grain?"

"The silo," answered another little girl.

"Right you are, Susie," praised the teacher. "And who can tell me what the little metal bird up on the roof is called? Class? How about you, Mark?"

"That's . . . uh . . . the weather thing."

"Close, Mark, very close. It is for telling us

something about the weather. But who can tell us what the exact name is, and why?"

"It's a weathercock," exclaimed Davey from the back row, "because if it were a weathercunt, the wind would blow right through it!"

•

Harry was delighted to encounter a young woman who accepted his proposal of marriage, as he was sensitive about his wooden leg and had been a bit afraid that no one would have him. In fact he couldn't quite bring himself to tell his fiancée about his leg when he slipped the engagement ring on her finger, nor when she bought the wedding dress, nor when they selected the time and place. All he kept saying was, "Darling, I've got a big surprise for you," at which she would blush and smile bewitchingly.

The wedding day finally arrived, and eventually the newlyweds found themselves alone in their hotel room. "Now don't forget, Harry, you promised me a big surprise," giggled the bride, slipping between the sheets.

Speechless now that the moment had arrived, Harry turned out the lights, unstrapped his artificial leg, got into bed, and placed his wife's hand on the stump.

"Hmmmm," she murmured, "that *is* a surprise. But pass me the Vaseline and I'll see what I can do."

•

What's 10, 9, 8, 7, 6, 5, 4, 3, 2, 1?
  Bo Derek getting older.

•

What do fat girls and mopeds have in common?
  They're both fun to ride until a friend sees you.

•

Fred's wife's refusal to wear underwear drove him crazy. He didn't think it was proper, or sanitary, but nothing he said persuaded her even to consider mending her ways. But when she fell ill one winter, Fred had a brainstorm. Calling up the family doctor, he said, "Doc, my wife's got a terrible cold and I wish you'd come over and take a look at her." He explained about her lack of underwear and went on to offer the doctor twice his usual fee if he could persuade the ornery woman that the illness was linked to her bad habit.

  The doctor came right over, and found the woman wrapped in a blanket on the living room sofa, coughing and blowing her nose. He proceeded to examine her and was looking down her throat when he spoke up. "Mrs. Brown, I'll give you some medication for this cold . . . but if you don't start wearing underwear, it could linger until spring."

"You mean to tell me, Doctor," asked the sick woman, "that you can tell by looking down my throat that I'm not wearing underpants?"

"That's right," he assured her.

"Well then, would you mind looking up my asshole and letting me know if my hat's on straight?"

•

Why do women have two holes so close together?

In case you miss.

•

If God hadn't meant us to eat pussy . . .

. . . He wouldn't have made it look like a taco.

•

A couple was lying in bed one morning, and the woman took it in mind to tell her companion about the dream she'd had the night before. "Honey, I dreamed I was at a cock auction," she recounted with a smile. "There were extra-large cocks going for $90 or so, medium-sized cocks selling for $50, and itty-bitty ones for $2.50."

"Say, was mine in the auction?" asked the man a bit anxiously.

"Darling, yours would've been too big to get in the door," she said reassuringly.

A few mornings later they were lying in bed again and the man spoke up. "You wouldn't believe what I dreamed last night. I was at a pussy auction. There were great big ones, and little hairy ones . . . oh, all kinds."

"Well, did you see mine?" she asked.

"Baby, the auction was *in* your pussy."

•

The divorce case was an especially acrimonious one, as the wife was suing on the grounds that her husband had failed to satisfy her needs. "Frankly," she advised the courtroom in a stage whisper, "he was so poorly endowed —and I mean *tiny*—that it just wasn't worth the effort."

The sympathetic judge awarded her a large settlement, and as she walked past her husband and his lawyer, she hissed, "Adios, sucker."

Sticking a finger in each corner of his mouth and pulling it as wide as possible, he replied, "So long, bitch."

•

What do soybeans and dildoes have in common?

They're both meat substitutes.

•

Did you hear about the bride who was so horny she carried a bouquet of batteries?

•

A young lady went out on a date with a young man she found quite attractive, so after dinner she invited him back to her apartment. Sitting him down on her couch with a drink, she proceeded to nibble on his ear, play with his hair, and so on, but the fellow only pulled up his collar and rubbed his hands together for warmth. The young lady pulled out all the stops, sitting on his lap, even directing his hands to appropriate portions of her anatomy. But he took no action whatsoever, even to the point of violently resisting her attempts to unbutton any of his garments.

Finally in desperation, after a particularly passionate embrace had met with no response, she blurted, "You know, I have a hole down there."

"Oh," responded the young man with evident relief, "so *that's* where the draft is coming from!"

•

Why do women like hunters?
Three reasons:
They go deep into the bush.
They always shoot twice.
And they always eat what they shoot.

•

Mrs. Jones was quite embarrassed when six-year-old Johnny burst into the bathroom, pointed at her pubic hair, and asked loudly, "What's that, Mommy?"

"That's my sponge, honey," she explained, thinking fast.

She was even more embarrassed when Johnny burst in a week later, because, to satisfy one of Mr. Jones's kinkier requests, she had shaved herself. In answer to Johnny's question, she hastily explained that she had lost her sponge. "It got dirty, honey," she told him, "and I threw it out the window."

Johnny was gone for a couple of hours, but returned with a big grin on his face. "I found your sponge, Mommy," he cried. "I looked in the Greens' window, and Mrs. Green was washing Mr. Green's face with it!"

•

Did you hear about the Italian girl who thought a sanitary belt was a drink from a clean shot glass?

•

How can you tell if a woman is wearing pantyhose?

If her ankles swell up when she farts.

•

Mel and Howie were regular fishing partners, but to Mel's irritation, Howie invariably had more luck. One Saturday morning they were out on the lake and Howie had already pulled in three nice-sized bass. Observing carefully, Mel noticed Howie sniffing his bait before putting it on the hook.

"How come?" he asked his friend.

"I have this med student friend," explained Howie, "who's always doing autopsies, and he slips me the pussies. The fish love 'em."

"I can see that," commented Mel enviously. "But why smell them?"

"Every so often he slips in an asshole."

•

What do eating pussy and dealing with the Mafia have in common?

One slip of the tongue and you're in deep shit.

•

Why did God give women nipples?

To make suckers out of men.

•

Three old ladies were sitting on a park bench when an exhibitionist walked up to them and displayed his endowments.

The first old lady had a stroke.

The second old lady had a stroke.

But the third old lady's arms were too short to reach.

•

How does a man know when he has eaten pussy well?

When he wakes up in the morning and his face looks like a glazed doughnut.

•

Bert and Ethel were debating whether they should get a house pet and, if so, what kind. At long last Bert decided a bear cub would be just the thing, but Ethel was skeptical. "Honey," she wondered aloud, "what'll it eat?"

"Bears eat anything," Bert pointed out. "We'll train him to eat at the table like us."

"But where will it go to the bathroom?"

"Bears are smart," Bert reassured her. "We'll train it to use the toilet."

"Okay, but where will the bear sleep?" worried Ethel.

"He can sleep with us," was Bert's solution.

"Sleep with us!" she shrieked. "But what about the hair? And the smell?"

"Now, now, Ethel," said Bert soothingly, "he'll get used to it—I did."

•

Three women are on the fast track at a certain company. The president decides it's time to promote one of them to an executive position. Unsure as to which woman to pick, he devises a little test. One day while they're all out at lunch, he places $500 on each of the women's desks.

Candidate #1 returns the money to him immediately.

Candidate #2 invests in the market and returns $1250 to him the next morning.

Candidate #3 pockets it.

So who gets the promotion? The one with the big tits!

•

Know the definition of a wife?

An attachment you screw on the bed to get the housework done.

•

What's the last sound you hear before a pubic hair hits the ground?

(Make a spitting sound.)

•

What's the difference between a hormone and an enzyme?
   You can't hear an enzyme.

•

So how do you make a hormone?
   Put sand in the vaseline.

•

Once the Bionic Woman had to take an overnight train trip. She entered her compartment without noticing that the berth above her was occupied by a young man. Peering through the curtains, he was quite chagrined to see her remove her wig, false eyelashes, glass eye, padded brassiere, mechanical hand, and bionic leg. When she got into bed and pulled up the covers, she caught sight of the peeping Tom and cried out in alarm, "Oh my goodness! What do you want?"

   "You know damn well what I want," he snarled. "Unscrew it and toss it up here."

•

When the newlywed couple checked into a remote lakeside hotel, the clerk and the bellhop exchanged broad winks in anticipation of the honeymoon hijinks to come. So they were quite surprised when, just before dawn of the couple's first night together, the new husband tromped down the stairs laden down with fishing gear. This happened again on the second night, and on the third, and finally the clerk and the bellhop could no longer contain their curiosity. "You're *fishing* at this ungodly hour on your honeymoon?" asked the bellhop. "Why aren't you up making love to your bride?"

The groom looked bewildered. "Make love to her? Oh, no, she's got gonorrhea."

Embarrassed silence. Then the desk clerk pointed out, "There's always oral sex."

"No way. She's got pyorrhea."

"I see. Well, what about anal sex?" suggested the bellhop helpfully.

"Nope. She's got diarrhea."

"Jesus." The clerk and the bellhop looked at the fellow with newborn sympathy. "So why on earth did you marry her?"

"Because she's got worms," explained the newlywed, "and I just *love* to fish."

•

First Woman: "This is very embarrassing, but every time I sneeze, I have an orgasm."
Second Woman: "You poor dear! Are you taking anything?"
First Woman: "Snuff."

•

Why did the New York Giants hire two nuns and a prostitute for the new season?

They needed two tight ends and a wide receiver.

●

I've got a joke so funny it'll make your tits fall off:

Oh . . . I see you've already heard it.

●

A young woman was terribly depressed because she was so flat-chested. So when her fairy godmother appeared one day and offered to grant her most heartfelt wish, the young woman instantly requested large breasts.

"All right, my dear," said her fairy godmother. "From this moment on, every time a man says 'Pardon' to you, your breasts will grow."

The next day the woman was walking down the sidewalk, lost in thought, when she bumped into a policeman. "Pardon me," said the cop politely.

Her tits grew an inch. She was ecstatic.

A few days later the young woman was doing her shopping at the supermarket. Coming out with a huge bag of groceries, she bumped into a delivery man and dropped them all over. "Oh, pardon me," he said, bending over to help her collect her purchases.

The young woman's tits grew another inch. She was beside herself with joy, and decided to treat herself to dinner at a Chinese restaurant. Going in the door, she collided with a waiter, who bowed and said, "Oh, missy, I beg of you a thousand pardons."

The next day the headlines read:

CHINESE WAITER KILLED BY TWO TORPEDOES.

•

What's the difference between a job and a wife?

After five years, the job still sucks.

•

Bumper sticker:

Support E.R.A. —Make *Him* Sleep on the Wet Spot

•

A young man had been in a bad accident and was told plastic surgery on his lip was necessary if he wanted to avoid being severely disfigured. Luckily the nurse had taken a fancy to him, and offered to donate skin. And since similar tissue was required, the doctor ended up grafting a piece of the nurse's pussy onto the fellow's mouth.

A year or so later, the doctor ran into his patient and was gratified to see that the injury was almost invisible. "How're you doing?" he asked.

"Can't complain. But Doc," confided the young man, "it's the weirdest thing—every time I take a leak, my lip quivers."

•

Farmer Sven was delighted that his new hired hand seemed to have uncommon intelligence and initiative, and so with a clear heart he decided to make a much-postponed business trip to the city. "I'll be gone for a week or so, Sal," he told the new man, "and I'm leaving everything in your hands."

Sal clapped him on the back and told him to rest easy, but greeted his employer with a long face upon his return. "Got some bad news, Sven," he admitted. "Know those eighteen prize heifers? Well, they got into the river somehow, and all but one drowned."

"Jeez," said Sven. "That's terrible. How's everything else?"

"Well, there was a fire in the barn, but we put it out before it reached the house."

"Jesus. I hope that's all the bad news."

"Not quite," admitted Sal. "Had a hailstorm and lost the whole crop."

"Oh my God." Farmer Sven sat down in the road. "Don't you have any good news?"

Sal brightened. "As a matter of fact, I do. Remember those nasty bleeding spells your

The teacher instructed her third-graders to pick a three-syllable word and to use it in a sentence. Several pupils raised their hands, including Dirty Petey, but the teacher passed him over. "Yes, Sally?"

"Beautiful," said Sally. "My teacher is beautiful."

"Why, thank you, Sally," praised the teacher, beaming. "Anyone else?" Again the teacher ignored Dirty Petey's hand. "Yes, Douglas?"

"Wonderful. My teacher is wonderful," offered Douglas.

"How very nice," said the teacher. This time she had no choice but to pick Dirty Petey.

"Urinate," said Petey brightly.

"Petey!" cried the teacher, shocked.

"Urinate," explained her pupil, "but if your tits were bigger you'd be a ten."

•

How many men does it take to mop a floor?
　None. It's a woman's job.

•

Two men meet on the commuter train and get to talking. The conversation moves from sports and the weather on to the subject of their wives. Says Fred, "You should know that my wife's actually pretty ugly."

"She may be no beauty," concedes Phil, "but my wife is probably the ugliest woman on the face of the earth."

They argue back and forth over which woman is uglier, and finally Fred figures out the only way to end the dispute. "You come on over to my house, Phil," he suggests to his new acquaintance, "and meet my old lady. If you still think your wife is uglier, we'll check her out."

So Phil agrees, and after a drink at home with Fred's wife, Fred pulls him aside. "Well?"

"I've got to admit that your wife is a real dog, but mine has her beat cold," says Phil. Fred is highly skeptical, but agrees to get back into the car and drive to Phil's. Phil leads Fred around through the back door, slides open a trap door, and yells, "Honey, I'm home. Come on up!"

A woman's voice calls back, "Do you want me to put the bag over my head?"

"No," Phil shouts back, "I don't want to screw you, I just want to show you to somebody!"

•

A guy and a girl are going at it hot and heavy on the sofa. "Put a finger inside me," she moans. "Another. Another. . . ." And so on until his whole hand's inside her. Pretty soon, following her passionate directives, he's in up to both elbows, and she whispers, "Put your head in." Obliging, he barely hears her instructions to crawl in.

So he's strolling around in there when he's startled by a voice out of the darkness asking "Who's there?" Another man comes up out of the shadows and asks, "What are *you* doing in here?"

"Just looking around," replies the first guy rather lamely.

"Well, if you find some keys, hand 'em over and we can ride my motorcycle out of here."

•

The substitute teacher was introducing herself to the class. "My name is Miss Prussy. "That's like 'pussycat,' only with an 'r'." The next morning she began the day by asking who remembered her name.

Little Johnny's hand shot up. "I do, I do—you're Miss Crunt."

•

A woman walked into a bar with a duck under her arm. One of the drunks at the bar looked over and commented, "That has got to be the ugliest pig I've ever seen."

"That's not a pig, it's a duck," said the woman indignantly.

The drunk explained, "I was talking to the duck."

Hear about the flaky geneticist in Southern California?

He's trying to cross a Mexican jumping bean with a cucumber, in order to create the world's first organic vibrator.

•

Some of his buddies decide to help out a fellow who's still a virgin, and very naive about sex. Pooling their funds, they hire a prostitute for their friend for the afternoon, unaware that she's had chili for lunch.

Because the guy is so inexperienced, she suggests some sixty-nine to start, and while they're going down on each other she can't hold in a giant, pungent fart. A few minutes later she lets out another one, right in his face.

That does it. The virgin jumps up and reaches for his pants, explaining, "It sure feels good, but I don't think I can take sixty-seven more of those farts!"

•

Why do women like to play Pac-Man?

Because they can get eaten three times for a quarter.

•

One day a certain housewife became extremely horny while going about the routine business of cleaning the house. Unfortunately her husband was still at work, so she resorted to stripping off all her clothes and masturbating furiously in the middle of the living room floor. She got pretty worked up, and was writhing and moaning when her husband walked in.

"Honey," he asked, looking up from the day's mail, "when you've finished vacuuming, could you get started on dinner?"

•

What were the most erotic words ever spoken on television?

"Gee, Ward, you were kind of rough on the Beaver last night."

•

What did the vampire say to the teacher?

"See you next period."

•

The horny husband was forever trying to talk his wife into having sex with him, usually unsuccessfully. One night, just before climbing into bed, he presented her with a glass of water and two aspirins.

"What's this, honey?" she asked. "I don't have a headache."

"Gotcha!"

•

Why don't girls wear dresses in the winter?

Chapped lips.

•

Why was the girl fired from her job at the sperm bank after she got pregnant?

They discovered she'd been embezzling.

•

Three men went for a ride in the country and their car broke down, so they went to the nearest farmhouse to ask for shelter. "Sure, fellahs," said the farmer, "you can spend the night here, but you've each got to spend the night with one of my daughters, 'cause they don't get much company out here." The visitors readily agreed, and during the night the farmer made the rounds to make sure each was going through with his end of the deal.

The next morning, after the overnight guests went on their way, the farmer called his daughters together. "Linda, why were you laughing last night?" he asked the eldest.

"Because it tickled, Daddy."

"Susie, why were you crying?"

"Because it hurt, Daddy."

"And Lizzie, why was there no noise at all from your room?"

"Because, Daddy, he told me not to talk with my mouth full."

•

"What would your mother say if she saw you doing this?" the social worker asked reproachfully.

"She'd kill me," answered the hooker. "I'm on her corner."

•

What's the ultimate in punk?

A pubic Mohawk.

•

A nice young woman made an appointment with a certain Dr. Armetta and asked him if it was true that he could make things grow. The doctor assured her that this was indeed the case, at which she blurted, "Please give me something to make my breasts larger; I can't go on living being so flat-chested."

"Easy enough," Dr. Armetta reassured her. "You must simply say, 'Mary had a little lamb' three times a day."

On her way home she stopped at the supermarket. In the frozen-foods aisle, after looking both ways to make sure she was alone, she said quickly, "Mary had a little lamb," then said a prayer. Suddenly a man stepped out from behind her and said, "I see you've been to Dr. Armetta, too."

"Why, yes," she stammered. "How did you know?"

The man unzipped his fly, pulled out his penis, and shouted, *"Hickory, dickory dock!"*

•

How can you tell when a girl is horny?

When you put your hand in her pants and it feels like a horse eating oats.

•

What are three things a woman can do that a man can't?

1) Have a baby.
2) Have her period.
3) Get laid when she's dead.

•

Did you hear about the two sailors and a nurse who were stranded together on a desert island?

After three months, the nurse was so disgusted with what she was doing that she killed herself.

After three more months, the sailors were so

disgusted with what they were doing that they buried her.

•

What's the difference between a young whore and an old whore?

The young whore uses K-Y jelly; the old whore uses Poli-Grip.

•

Hungry after overseeing the delivery of his cattle to a Chicago stockyard, a cowboy headed for a nearby restaurant for dinner. The only vacant seat was next to a young, wealthy, well-educated young lady, and the cowboy couldn't help but overhear her placing her order: "I'll have a breast of fowl, virgin fowl. Make sure it's a virgin—catch it yourself. Garnish my plate with onions, and bring me a cup of coffee, not too hot and not too cold. Oh, and waiter, open the window. I smell horse; there must be a cowboy in the house."

Thoroughly pissed off, the cowboy proceeded to place his own order: "I'll have a duck, fucked—fuck it yourself. Garnish my plate with horseshit, then bring me a cup of coffee as strong as Texas mule piss, and blow the foam off with a fart. Oh, and waiter, knock down the wall. I smell cunt; there must be a whore in the house."

What's the ultimate in embarrassment for a woman?

Taking her German Shepherd to the vet and finding out it has the clap.

•

A mother and daughter lived together in devastating poverty, so it was cause for great rejoicing when the daughter found fifty cents on the sidewalk one day. She ran home and showed the coins to her mother, who decided that for fifty cents they could get two eggs and a bottle of ketchup and have a real meal. So off went the girl to the store.

As luck would have it, the daughter was happily skipping home with the eggs and ketchup when a truck backfired, startling her so much that she dropped the groceries. Staring down at the ruined feast, which was smashed at her feet, she burst into tears.

A passerby came up behind her and surveyed the scene. "Aw, honey, don't cry," he consoled her. "It would have died anyway: its eyes were too far apart."

•

Why is a clitoris like Antarctica?

Most men know it's down there, but few really care.

What's the best thing about Women's Liberation?

It gives you girls something to do in your spare time.

•

A young woman walked into a pharmacy and asked the pharmacy for a gross of rubbers. Figuring that an order of that size deserved a snappy answer, the pharmacist quipped, "What size would you like?"

"Oh, mix 'em up," she told him. "I'm not going steady."

•

An employee of a factory that manufactured all sorts of rubber goods was giving some guests a factory tour. Of special interest was the condom plant, where rubbers were being peeled off penis-shaped molds and rolled up for packaging. But every twelfth one was pulled off the production line by a worker who punched a small hole in the tip.

Shocked, one of the visitors exclaimed, "What are you doing? Think of all the unwanted pregnancies that's going to cause!"

"Yeah," agreed the employee with a shrug, "but it sure helps the nipple division."

•

Sadly neglected by her husband, a horny housewife turned to her next-door neighbor for advice. "Why don't you order some stuff from your milkman," was her suggestion, "and when the bill comes, you can settle it with sex?"

This seemed like an excellent idea, not least because the milkman was young and cute, and sure enough, when the bill was presented the milkman was delighted to settle for a long and energetic screw. Pulling his uniform back on, he reached for the bill to mark it "Paid in Full."

"Oh, no you don't," screeched the housewife, grabbing it out of his hand. "You brought me the milk a quart at a time, and that's the way I'm gonna pay for it."

•

After going through Lamaze, LeBoyer, and La Leche classes with his expectant wife, the proud new father remained by his wife's bedside throughout the labor and birth, bonding with the newborn child. Wanting to be as sympathetic and sensitive as possible, he took his wife's hand and said emotionally, "Tell me, darling, how was it? How did it actually feel to give birth?"

"Smile," his wife instructed. "Smile as hard as you can."

Beaming beatifically at his wife and newborn son, the father commented, "That's not so hard."

She continued, "Now stick your fingers in the corners of your mouth." He obeyed, still smiling broadly.

"Now stretch your lips as wide as they'll go," his wife ordered.

"Still not too tough," he said.

"Now pull them over your head."

•

"When my husband climaxes," the woman complained to the marriage counselor, "his reaction includes an ear-shattering yell."

"All things considered," commented the counselor, "I'd think that might be a source of some satisfaction for you."

"Oh, it would be," she said, "if it just didn't wake me up."

•

A good-looking woman walked into a bar and ordered a Michelob Light. It tasted so good that she ordered another, and another, and another, until she passed out cold. Several truck drivers had been observing her progress with interest, and they promptly took her into the back room and energetically screwed her.

Early the next morning the woman came to and made her way home. But that evening she reappeared, ordered a series of Michelob

Lights, and got so drunk that the truck drivers again had their way with her unconscious form.

This went on for several more nights, until one evening when the woman showed up at the bar and ordered a Miller Lite. By now hers was a familiar face, so the bartender asked why she'd decided to switch brands.

Leaning across the bar, she confided, "Michelob makes my pussy hurt."

•

What do you call a four-foot woman in the Navy?
A microwave.

•

As the newlywed couple was checking into the hotel for their honeymoon, another couple at the desk offered to show them around the town that night. Thanking them for the kind offer, the bridegroom explained that it was their wedding night and that they'd prefer to take a rain check.

When the second couple came down to breakfast the next morning they were astonished to catch sight of the groom in the hotel bar apparently drowning his sorrows. "Why, you should be the happiest man in the world today," they said, coming over to him.

"Yesterday I was," said the man mournfully,

"but this morning, without realizing it, I put three ten-dollar bills on the pillow and got up to get dressed."

"Hey, cheer up, she probably didn't even notice."

"That's the problem," the groom went on. "Without even thinking, she gave me five dollars change."

•

Fred came home from work in time to catch his wife sliding naked down the bannister. "What the hell are you doing?" he demanded.

"Just heating up dinner, darling," she cried.

•

Definition of vagina:
  The box a penis comes in.

•

How do you start a fire without any matches?
  Hold a piece of toilet paper behind a fat girl wearing corduroys.

•

A pretty woman moved into town. She was so resistant to any advances by the local menfolk that they decided there must be something wrong with her sexual apparatus—maybe that she was a hermaphrodite. One guy finally talked her into going out to a movie with him, and was delighted when on the drive back she explained she urgently had to go to the bathroom. As she squatted in the bushes beside the car, he figured this was his chance to check out her anatomy, and snuck around the rear. Sure enough something hung down between her legs, and he reached out and grabbed it. "So!" he exclaimed weakly.

"You didn't tell me you were a peeping Tom," she said tartly.

"And you didn't tell me you had to take a shit!"

●

What's red, lives in a cave, and only comes out during sex?

(Stick out your tongue.)

●

What's the difference between worry and panic?

About twenty-eight days.

●

A certain virginal and shy college freshman was lucky to have a roommate who was considerably more experienced. When the bashful boy broke down and explained his predicament, his roommate was quick to offer to set him up with the campus floozie. "Just take her out to dinner and a show and then let nature take its course," he explained reassuringly. "This girl knows what the score is."

The roommate arranged the date as promised, and the freshman took the coed out for a delightful evening of dining and dancing. On the way home he parked his car in a dark lane, broke out in a cold sweat, and blurted out, "Gosh, I sure would love to have a little pussy."

"I would too," she sighed. "Mine's the size of a milk pail."

●

During intercourse a husband had a heart attack and died. The next day the mortician informed the wife that the corpse still had a hard-on and he thought it would look odd in the coffin. "You've got a point," agreed the widow. "Cut it off and stick it up his ass."

Making absolutely sure he'd heard correctly, the mortician obeyed her instructions. During the funeral a number of the deceased's friends and relations were perturbed to see a tear in the corner of his eye, but the widow assured them there was no cause for concern.

Just before the casket was closed, she leaned over and quietly whispered in her dead husband's ear, "It *hurts*, doesn't it?"

●

A man called his wife from the hospital to tell her he'd cut his finger off at the assembly line. "Oh, honey," she cried, "the whole finger?"

"No," he said, "the one next to it."

●

An old lech walked into a bar and ordered a whiskey. "What kind of whiskey, sir?" asked the bartender politely.

"I take my whiskey like I take my women," was the answer, "twelve years old."

●

Definition of an orgasm:
  Gland finale.

●

In Dallas on business, Jerry picked up a lovely girl in the hotel bar and took her up to his room. After a few drinks, the girl sat on his lap. "Would you like to hug me?" she asked.

"Of course," panted Jerry, pulling her close.

"And would you like to kiss me?"

"You bet," said Jerry, planting a long kiss on her lips.

"Okay, honey," she continued, "brace yourself, because here comes the fifty-dollar question."

●

What's the difference between an Italian woman and Bigfoot?

One is six feet tall, covered with matted hair, and smells terrible; the other has big feet.

•

A gigolo marries an ugly, none-too-bright woman who happens to have loads of money. One day the man goes out to repair a hole in the roof of the stable. "I'll need a ladder," he tells his wife.

"Get the ladder, get the ladder," she repeats dutifully as she trots off.

"I'll need a hammer and nails," he says a bit later.

"Get the hammer, get the nails, get the hammer . . ." she murmurs as she runs back to the tool shed.

The guy gets down to work and is hammering away when he hits himself squarely on the thumb. "FUCK!" he screams.

His wife bobs away, muttering, "Get the bag, get the bag!"

•

A man and his wife were fooling around when she asked, "Honey, could you take your ring off? It's hurting me."

Her husband replies, "Ring, hell! That's my wristwatch."

This woman goes to the gynecologist for the first time and is rather embarrassed by the whole setup. Instructing her to put her feet in the stirrups, the doctor goes around for a look. "Why, that's the biggest pussy I've ever seen," he exclaims, "the biggest pussy I've ever seen!"

"You didn't have to say it twice," snaps the woman.

"I didn't," says the doctor.

•

Why is rape so rare?

Because a woman can run faster with her dress up than a man with his pants down.

•

A Texan comes into a bar and it only takes him a few drinks to start boasting about the superior size of just about everything in Texas. "Did you know our women have tits forty feet across?" he asks proudly.

"Oh, really," says the man next to him politely.

"Well, they only miss it by this much," allows the Texan, holding his fingers about two inches apart. "And our women have cunts so big they can hold a dick twenty feet long."

"No kidding."

"Well not quite, but they only miss it by

about this much," says the Texan, indicating another two inches.

"Say, I bet you didn't know that the women in these parts have babies out their assholes," offers the local man.

"Is that so!" says the Texan, astonished.

"Well not really, but they only miss it by about this much . . ."

•

What's the worst thing about having a cold when you've got your period?

Having your tampon pop out when you sneeze.

•

Know how to make a pussy talk?

Put a tongue in it.

•

A nymphomaniac goes to the supermarket and gets all hot and bothered eyeing the carrots and cucumbers. By the time she gets to the checkout line she can't hold out much longer, so she asks one of the supermarket baggers to carry her groceries out to the car for her. They're halfway across the lot when the nympho slips her hand down his pants and whispers, "You know, I've got an itchy pussy."

"Sorry, lady," says the bagger, "but I can't tell one of those Japanese cars from another."

•

Where do women airline pilots sit?
    In the cuntpit.

•

What's the definition of a metallurgist?
    A man who can tell if a platinum blonde is a virgin metal or a common ore.

•

Little Red Riding Hood was strolling through the woods on the way to visit her grandmother when suddenly the Big Bad Wolf jumped out from behind a tree. Licking his sharp white teeth, he snarled ferociously, "Now little girl, I'm going to eat you all up!"

"Eat, eat, eat!" snapped Little Red Riding Hood disgustedly. "Doesn't anyone fuck any more?"

Or maybe you prefer this version:

Little Red Riding Hood was strolling through the woods on the way to visit her grandmother when suddenly the Big Bad Wolf jumped out from behind a tree. Licking his sharp white teeth, he snarled ferociously,

"Now little girl, I'm going to fuck you to death!"

"Oh no, you're not," snapped Little Red Riding Hood, pulling a .357 Magnum from her straw basket. "You're going to eat me first, just like the story says!"

•

Why did the woman with the huge pussy douche with Crest?

She heard it reduces cavities.

•

What's the difference between a woman and a volcano?

Volcanoes don't fake eruptions.

•

Two whores are walking down the street when one remarks, "I smell cock!"

The other replies, "That's just my breath."

•

A wife arriving home from a shopping trip was horrified to find her husband in bed with a lovely young thing. Just as she was about to storm out of the house, her husband stopped her with these words: "Before you leave, I want you to hear how this all came about. While I was driving along the highway, I saw this young girl here, looking tired and bedraggled, so I brought her home and made her a meal from the roast beef you had forgotten in the refrigerator. She had only some worn-out sandals on her feet, so I gave her a pair of good shoes you'd discarded because they had gone out of style. She was cold, so I gave her the sweater I bought you for your birthday that you never wore because the colors didn't suit you. Her jeans were worn out, so I gave her a pair of yours that were perfectly good but too small for you now," the husband went on. "Then, as she was about to leave the house, she paused and asked, 'Is there anything else your wife doesn't use anymore?' "

•

A newlywed couple was en route to the resort where they were to spend their honeymoon when the bride was seized by a desperate need to pee. "Aw, honey, we're almost there," Ken pointed out. "Can you hold out just a little longer?"

Vicky agreed, but about ten minutes later she said, "Baby, I really gotta go." Assuring her the hotel was only a few miles further, Ken drove on.

A few minutes later the desperate bride begged her husband to stop the car. "Then roll down the window and pee," he told her sternly. "I'm not stopping till we get there."

Two hitchhikers were standing over the crest of the next hill, and just as the car passed, Vicky let go out the window, drenching one of them. "Jeez, didja see that guy spit in my face?" the hitchhiker sputtered, trying to wipe himself off.

"That's nothing," responded his friend. "You should have seen his lips!"

•

A woman went to the gynecologist and was told she was in perfect health, with the body of an eighteen-year-old. She was so excited she ran home to tell her husband.

"Oh yeah?" he said snidely. "What about your fat ass?"

"He didn't say anything about you."

•

Bumper sticker: Save the Whale—Harpoon a Fat Chick.

•

Mrs. Jones was quite startled when her six-year-old son barged into the bathroom just as she was stepping out of the shower. She hastily covered up, but not before the little boy had pointed right at her crotch and asked, "What's that?"

"Oh," she said, thinking fast, "that's where I got hit with an axe."

"Got you right in the cunt, didn't it?"

•

Why's virginity like a balloon?

One prick and they're both gone.

•

One summer evening in New York a pretty girl was walking across Broadway and was hit by a truck. The impact was so strong that she flew up into the air, and by the time she hit the ground all her clothes had been stripped away.

As a crowd started to gather, a passing priest who had witnessed the accident rushed over and placed his hat over the victim's crotch so as to preserve a little decency.

Soon a drunkard, wondering what was going on, staggered through the crowd and caught sight of the naked girl lying in the street, covered only by the priest's hat. "Oh Christ," he mumbled, "first thing we have to do is get that man out of there."

•

Why are pregnant women like defective type-writers?

They skip their periods.

•

What's the definition of feminine deodorant spray?
   Around-the-cock protection.

•

What's an 11?
   A 10 who swallows.

Would you like to see your favorite tasteless jokes in print? If so, send them to:

Blanche Knott
c/o St. Martin's Press
175 Fifth Avenue
New York, NY 10010

We're sorry to say that no compensation or credit can be given. But I *love* hearing from my tasteless readers.

B. K.